The Crash of the Hindenburg

By Justine Dunn

Scott Foresman
is an imprint of

Glenview, Illinois • Boston, Massachusetts • Chandler, Arizona •
Upper Saddle River, New Jersey

Photographs

Every effort has been made to secure permission and provide appropriate credit for photographic material. The publisher deeply regrets any omission and pledges to correct errors called to its attention in subsequent editions.

Unless otherwise acknowledged, all photographs are the property of Pearson Education, Inc.

Photo locators denoted as follows: Top (T), Center (C), Bottom (B), Left (L), Right (R), Background (Bkgd)

Opener: (Bkgd) ©Bettman/Corbis, (CL) ©David R. Frazier Photolibrary, Inc./Alamy Images, (CR) ©idp manchester airport collection/Alamy; **1** Keystone/Getty Images; **3** (Inset) ©AP Photo, (Bkgd) ©National Aviation Museum/Corbis; **4** (Inset) AKG London Ltd., (Bkgd) Central Press/Hulton Archive/Getty Images; **6** AKG London Ltd.; **7** ©The Granger Collection, NY; **8** ©AP Photo; **9** (Bkgd) ©Bettman/Corbis, (CL) ©David R. Frazier Photolibrary, Inc./Alamy Images, (CR) ©idp manchester airport collection/Alamy; **10** AKG London Ltd.; **12** Keystone/Getty Images; **13** ©AP Photo; **14** ©Bettmann/Corbis; **15** ©Austrian Archives/Corbis.

ISBN 13: 978-0-328-47270-3
ISBN 10:   0-328-47270-0

Copyright © by Pearson Education, Inc., or its affiliates. All rights reserved. Printed in the United States of America. This publication is protected by copyright, and permission should be obtained from the publisher prior to any prohibited reproduction, storage in a retrieval system, or transmission in any form or by any means, electronic, mechanical, photocopying, recording, or likewise. For information regarding permissions, write to Pearson Curriculum Rights & Permissions, One Lake Street, Upper Saddle River, New Jersey 07458.

Pearson® is a trademark, in the U.S. and/or in other countries, of Pearson plc or its affiliates.
Scott Foresman® is a trademark, in the U.S. and/or in other countries, of Pearson Education, Inc., or its affiliates.

Zeppelin's rigid airship

Count Ferdinand von Zeppelin

In 1900 a German man named Count Ferdinand von Zeppelin invented the first rigid airship.

You may have seen one of these airships over a large holiday parade or a football game on TV. They're also known as blimps, or zeppelins, after their inventor.

Zeppelin had taken a ride in a hot-air balloon. But a hot-air balloon is guided by the wind. He wanted to invent an airship that a pilot could steer.

Dirigible is another word for airship. It means "able to be steered" in German.

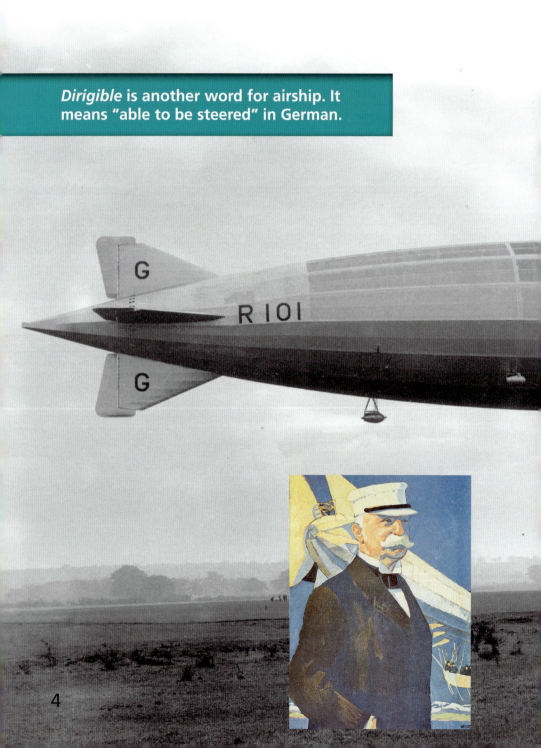

Zeppelin designed an airship, or **dirigible**, with large balloons inside it. The balloons were filled with **hydrogen**. Hydrogen is a very lightweight gas, so it rises easily. But it's also very **flammable**.

At first, dirigibles were used to carry people across Germany. Later, the Germans used them to drop bombs during World War I.

Early dirigibles were used to transport people.

When the war was over, the Germans began to build more dirigibles to carry passengers. They could cross the Atlantic Ocean much faster than steamships. But they were still very dangerous because of the hydrogen inside them.

A German brochure advertising traveling on a dirigible

The Germans needed a lightweight gas that wouldn't burn. Their plan was to fill the balloons in the *Hindenburg* with helium instead of hydrogen. This gas could still lift the heavy dirigible and the people on board, and it was much, much safer than hydrogen.

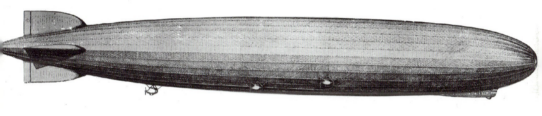

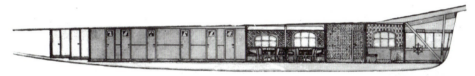
Längsschnitt

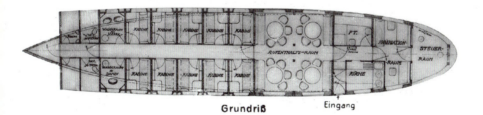
Grundriß   Eingang

A dirigible contains several large bags filled with gas.

It took five years for the Germans to build the *Hindenburg*. It was the largest airship ever built. It was 804 feet long and 135 feet wide. That's three times longer than today's jets!

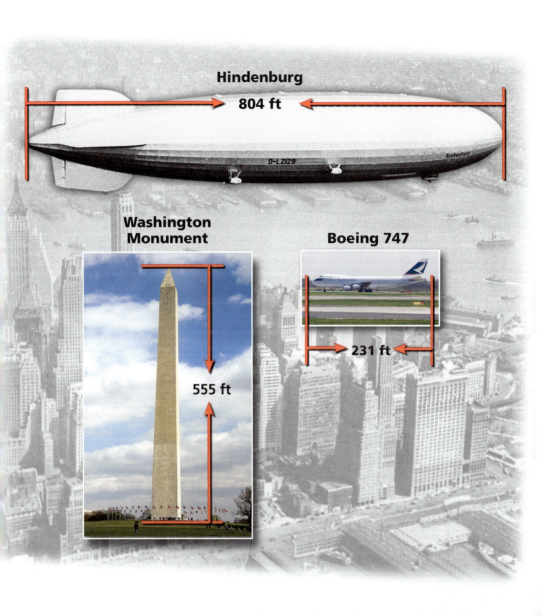

If you stood the *Hindenburg* on its end, it would be taller than the Washington Monument!

The *Hindenburg* was very fancy inside. It had guest rooms, a dance floor, and a dining room. A ticket to cross the Atlantic Ocean cost $400. At the time, you could buy a new car for that much money!

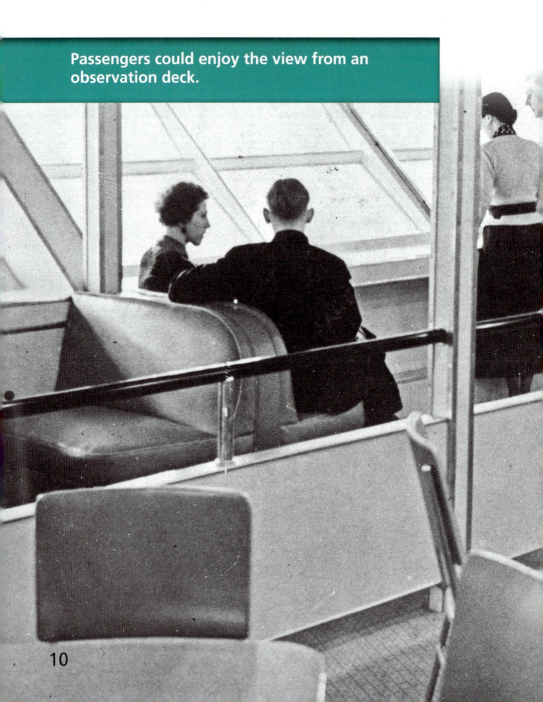

Passengers could enjoy the view from an observation deck.

One room in the *Hindenburg* had a special door and fireproof walls. It even had a guard! In the room was a table with an electric lighter attached to a cord. In those days, many people smoked. To prevent fires, passengers could smoke in this room only.

The *Hindenburg* over New Jersey

On May 3, 1937, the *Hindenburg* left Germany for its first trip to the United States that year. There were 36 passengers and 61 crew members on board. On the last day of the trip, the airship ran into a bad storm, which delayed its landing. Finally, at about 7:00 PM on May 6, the *Hindenburg* was over the landing field in New Jersey. No one expected what happened next.

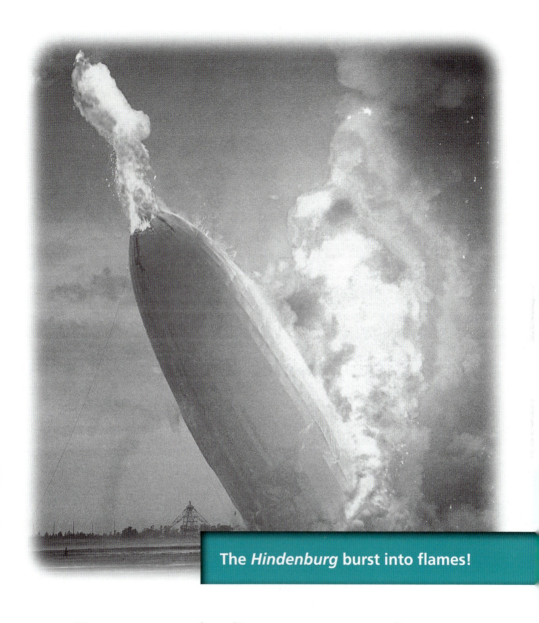

The *Hindenburg* burst into flames!

Newspaper and radio reporters were there to watch the *Hindenburg* arrive. They watched as the crew dropped ropes to the ground. Suddenly, the tail of the dirigible burst into flames! It took only seconds for the ship to fall to the ground in a ball of fire.

Thirty-six people died in the fiery crash. We still don't know what caused the fire. Some people blamed the weather. Others blamed static electricity. Some people thought it was **sabotage**.

The cause of the disaster is still unknown.

It cost a lot of money to build the *Hindenburg*. Some of the money came from Adolf Hitler and the Nazi party. Many Germans hated Hitler, though. Did one of the passengers or one of the crew hide a bomb on the airship? We may never know.

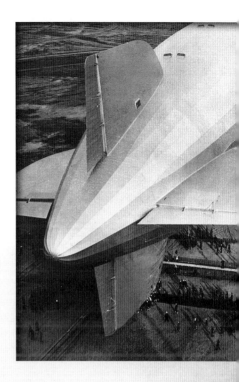

Glossary

dirigible *n.* an airship with its own power and steering

flammable *adj.* easily set on fire

helium *n.* a lightweight gas that does not burn

hydrogen *n.* a lightweight gas that burns easily

rigid *adj.* something that does not bend; stiff

sabotage *n.* destruction of something on purpose, in a secretive manner